Wouldn't it be a nice thing to have a curious dream, just like Alice? The best plan is this. First lie down under a tree, and wait till a White Rabbit runs by, with a watch in his hand: then shut your eyes, and pretend to be dear little Alice.

—THE NURSERY ALICE, 1890

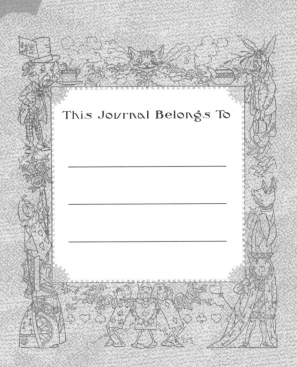

This Journal Belongs To

_____

_____

_____

Dreaming: A Journey Down the Magical Rabbit Hole

As you begin to record your dreams in this journal, try and remember to record not only what *happened* in your dream, but also how you *felt* throughout the events. The emotions you experience in your dreams often represent the most important aspect of dream journaling.

Whether you experience anxiety, fear, or happiness in your dreams, your emotions tend to reflect how you feel throughout the days' events. If you can learn to record and describe these emotions from your dreams, you may begin to see patterns between your dreaming life and waking life.

As you become more skilled at remembering your dreams (practice makes perfect!), you should start to make note of your other senses: what did you smell, taste, hear, and touch? By making a conscious effort to remember these details, your entries will become even more vivid and revealing. You will become more adept at identifying elements from your daily life that recur in a different form in your dreams and more attuned to how you react to situations and people in your life.

Keeping track of your dreams is an important part of being self-aware, so keep your journal and pen nearby—and happy dreaming!

Sleep Quiz-z-z-z . . .

Take a moment to answer the following questions about your sleeping patterns. You may notice some links between your daily (and nightly) routine and your dreaming patterns.

How many hours of sleep do you generally get each night?

Do you have a consistent sleep schedule?

Do you often fall asleep soon after eating?

Do you wake up for midnight snacks?

Do you remember your dreams more during

○ weeknights?

○ weekend nights?

○ naps?

Quick Tips

~ Always keep your dream journal and a pen near your bed (and maybe a flashlight or lamp as well).

~ Think about the events of the day before falling asleep. What did you do? Who did you see? How did you feel? You may be surprised by what appears in your dreams that night.

~ Record your dreams in the present tense rather than the past to allow your recollections to flow more fluidly.

~ Read articles and books about dreams and dream symbolism to increase your knowledge.

~ Include sketches and illustrations in your journal if you feel inspired.

~ Get enough sleep. If you are tired, you tend to sleep too deeply and will have trouble remembering your dreams when you wake up.

"Begin at the beginning," the King said gravely, "and go on till you come to the end: then stop."

—ALICE'S ADVENTURES IN WONDERLAND, 1865

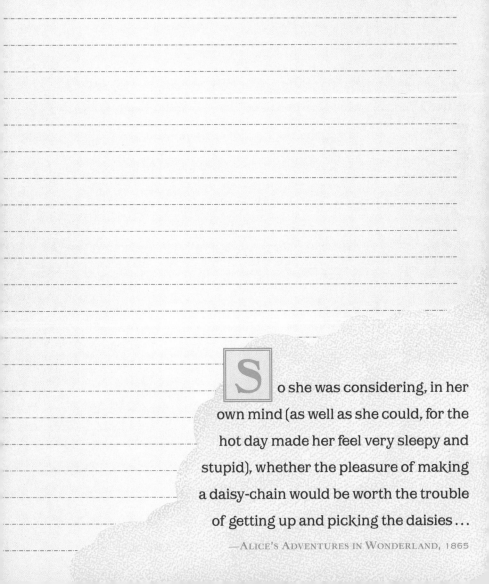

S o she was considering, in her own mind (as well as she could, for the hot day made her feel very sleepy and stupid), whether the pleasure of making a daisy-chain would be worth the trouble of getting up and picking the daisies...

—ALICE'S ADVENTURES IN WONDERLAND, 1865

date:

date:

date:

After such a fall as this, I shall think nothing of tumbling down-stairs! How brave they'll all think me at home!

—ALICE'S ADVENTURES IN WONDERLAND, 1865

date:

date:

Dream
symbol: FALL

To dream you fall from a high place . . . denotes loss of place and goods; if you are in love, it surely indicates that you will never marry the present object of your affection.

—THE VICTORIAN BOOK OF DREAMS

date:

date:

The Rabbit started violently, dropped
the white kid-gloves and the fan,
and scurried away into the
darkness as hard as he could go.

—ALICE'S ADVENTURES IN WONDERLAND, 1865

date:

Dream symbol: GLOVES

To dream that you lose your
right-hand glove denotes the
death of your wife (or husband).
To dream of losing both your
gloves implies failure and
bankruptcy and sorrow.

—THE VICTORIAN BOOK OF DREAMS

date:

date:

date:

date:

Curiouser and curiouser!

—ALICE'S ADVENTURES IN WONDERLAND, 1865

Mad as a Hatter

Some dreams are so bizarre that you wake up startled by the fantastic inventions of your own mind. Jot down memories of some of your most unusual trips down the rabbit hole.

date:

"How do you know I'm mad?"
said Alice. "You must be,"
said the Cat, "or you wouldn't
have come here."

—ALICE'S ADVENTURES IN WONDERLAND, 1865

date:

date:

date:

Dream
symbol: MAD

To dream you are mad, and
that you are in company with
mad people, is very good
to the dreamer; it promises
long life, riches, happy
marriage, success in trade,
and good children.

—THE VICTORIAN BOOK OF DREAMS

date:

date:

date:

date:

date:

date:

date:

date:

Oh dear, what nonsense I'm talking!

—ALICE'S ADVENTURES IN WONDERLAND, 1865

Pillow Talk

Have you ever been told that you talk in your sleep? Keep a list of things you have supposedly said.

date:

Y ou might just as well say," added the Dormouse, who seemed to be talking in his sleep, "that 'I breathe when I sleep' is the same thing as 'I sleep when I breathe'!"

—ALICE'S ADVENTURES IN WONDERLAND, 1865

date:

date:

date:

date:

date:

Twinkle, twinkle, little bat!

How I wonder what you're at!

Up above the world you fly,

Like a tea tray in the sky.

Twinkle, twinkle ——

—*Mad Hatter*,
ALICE'S ADVENTURES IN WONDERLAND, 1865

Dream
symbol: SINGING

It is an unfavourable omen to dream that you are singing, as it is generally the forerunner of bad and melancholy intelligence.... To dream that you hear others singing prognosticates good news, success in your undertakings, robust health, and long life; also a happy marriage with a good-tempered partner.

—THE VICTORIAN BOOK OF DREAMS

date:

date:

date:

date:

date:

date:

Queens never make bargains.

—*The Red Queen*, THROUGH THE LOOKING-GLASS
AND WHAT ALICE FOUND THERE, 1872

date:

Dream
symbol: QUEEN

To dream that you are in the
presence of the Queen denotes
that you will rise to great honour,
and will occupy a very important
situation in life. To a young woman
it shows that she will marry a person holding a good Government
situation, and ... they will be very
rich and happy, and live in great
grandeur and pomp.

—THE VICTORIAN BOOK OF DREAMS

date:

date:

date:

date:

date:

lice laughed.
"There's no use in trying," she said,
"one *can't* believe impossible things."
"I daresay you haven't had much
practice," said the Queen. "When I was
your age, I always did it for half-an-hour
a day. Why, sometimes I've believed as many
as six impossible things before breakfast."

—THROUGH THE LOOKING-GLASS
AND WHAT ALICE FOUND THERE, 1872

date:

date:

date:

date:

date:

date:

She was getting so used to
queer things happening.

—ALICE'S ADVENTURES IN WONDERLAND, 1865

Recurring Dreams

Do you have dreams that occur again and again? Keep track of repeating themes and question the significance of these particular dreams in your life.

date:

For, you see, so many out-of-the-way things had happened lately, that Alice had begun to think that very few things were really impossible.

—ALICE'S ADVENTURES IN WONDERLAND, 1865

date:

date:

date:

date:

date:

"I beg your pardon?" said Alice.

"It isn't respectable to beg," said the King.

—THROUGH THE LOOKING GLASS
AND WHAT ALICE FOUND THERE, 1872

date:

Dream

symbol: KING

To dream of a king

denotes strife and

slavery of the mind.

—THE VICTORIAN BOOK OF DREAMS

date:

date:

date:

date:

date:

date:

date:

The Caterpillar and Alice looked at each other

for some time in silence: at last

the Caterpillar took the hookah out of its mouth,

and addressed her in a languid, sleepy voice.

—ALICE'S ADVENTURES IN WONDERLAND, 1865

date:

date:

date:

date:

"Who are *you*?" said the Caterpillar.

—ALICE'S ADVENTURES IN WONDERLAND, 1865

Guest Appearances

Sometimes figures you have not thought about for years will make a surprise appearance in your dreams. Make a list of random people (an old classmate, crush, neighbor, or friend) who have recently visited you in your dreams.

date:

I wish you wouldn't keep
appearing and vanishing so suddenly:
you make one quite giddy!

—ALICE'S ADVENTURES IN WONDERLAND, 1865

date:

date:

date:

When I used to read fairy-tales, thought Alice, I fancied that kind of thing never happened, and now here I am in the middle of one!

—ALICE'S ADVENTURES IN WONDERLAND, 1865

date:

date:

date:

A large rose-tree stood near the entrance of the garden:

the roses growing on it were white, but there were three

gardeners at it, busily painting them red.

—ALICE'S ADVENTURES IN WONDERLAND, 1865

date:

Dream
symbol: ROSES

Nothing can be more favourable

than to dream of these

beautiful flowers, as they are

certain emblems of happiness,

prosperity, and long life.

—THE VICTORIAN BOOK OF DREAMS

date:

date:

date:

date:

Alice . . . always took a great interest
in questions of eating and drinking.

—ALICE'S ADVENTURES IN WONDERLAND, 1865

Do you have
particularly lucid
dreams after eating
decadent desserts,
or vivid nightmares
after spicy dinners?
What types of food
and drink trigger
a night of colorful
dreaming for you?

date:

Maybe it's always pepper that
makes people hot-tempered....
and vinegar that makes them sour—
and chamomile that makes them bitter—
and—and barley-sugar and such things
that make children sweet-tempered.

—ALICE'S ADVENTURES IN WONDERLAND, 1865

date:

If you drink much from a bottle
marked "poison," it is almost certain
to disagree with you, sooner or later.

—ALICE'S ADVENTURES IN WONDERLAND, 1865

date:

Dream
symbol: EATING

To dream that you are eating is

a very unfavourable omen; it

portends disunion amongst

your family, losses in trade, and

disappointment in love.

—THE VICTORIAN BOOK OF DREAMS

date:

date:

date:

date:

date:

date:

But if I'm not the same, the next question is, Who in the world am I?

—ALICE'S ADVENTURES IN WONDERLAND, 1865

Shape-Shifter

Have you ever changed into someone (or something) else in the middle of your dream? List these altered identities and think about whether they relate to your real-life aspirations.

date:

How puzzling all these changes are! I'm never sure what I'm going to be, from one minute to another!

—ALICE'S ADVENTURES IN WONDERLAND, 1865

date:

date:

date:

date:

date:

date:

Sweet Dreams

It is always difficult to wake up from a wonderful dream.
Record a few reveries that you wish would come true.

_____

_____

_____

_____

_____

_____

_____

_____

_____

S o Alice got up and
ran off, thinking while she ran,
as well she might, what a wonderful
dream it had been.

—ALICE'S ADVENTURES IN WONDERLAND, 1865

Night Screams

It is always a relief to wake up from nightmares. Make a list of
disturbing dreams you hope never to experience again.

The Queen had only one
way of settling all difficulties,
great or small. "Off with his head!"
she said, without even looking around.

—ALICE'S ADVENTURES IN WONDERLAND, 1865

date:

date:

date:

date:

date:

date:

date:

"Who cares for you?" said Alice
(she had grown to her full size by this time).
"You're nothing but a pack of cards!"

—ALICE'S ADVENTURES IN WONDERLAND, 1865

date:

Dream
symbol: CARDS

To dream you are playing at cards is a sure prognostic that you will be in love and speedily married.... If your cards are mostly diamonds, the person you will marry will be of a sour and disagreeable temper; if they are mostly hearts, your marriage will cement love, and you will be very happy and have many children; if they are mostly clubs, you will get money by your marriage; if they are mostly spades, your marriage will turn out very unhappy, and your children will be undutiful.

—THE VICTORIAN BOOK OF DREAMS

date:

date:

date:

date:

date:

date:

date:

Well! I've often seen
a cat without a grin,
thought Alice;
but a grin
without a cat!
It's the most curious
thing I ever saw
in all my life!

—ALICE'S ADVENTURES IN
WONDERLAND, 1865

date:

Dream symbol: CATS

It is exceedingly unfavourable to dream of cats, as they at once imply treachery and deceit. If a young woman dreams of cats, she may depend that her lover is deceiving her: and if a young man, rely upon it his lady love is a vixen in temper and disposition.

—THE VICTORIAN BOOK OF DREAMS

date:

date:

date:

date:

date:

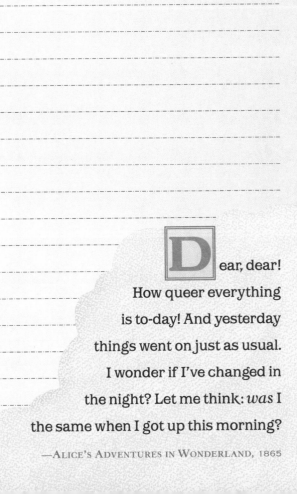

Dear, dear!
How queer everything
is to-day! And yesterday
things went on just as usual.
I wonder if I've changed in
the night? Let me think: *was* I
the same when I got up this morning?

—ALICE'S ADVENTURES IN WONDERLAND, 1865

date:

date:

date:

date:

date:

date:

date:

date:

"Wake up, Alice dear!"
said her sister;
"Why, what a long
sleep you've had!"

—ALICE'S ADVENTURES
IN WONDERLAND, 1865

POTTER STYLE

Design by MAGGIE HINDERS with LAURA PALESE
All illustrations by John Tenniel from the original *Alice's Adventures in Wonderland* (*AIW*),
London: Macmillan,1865, except: COVER: E. Gertrude Thomson, *The Nursery Alice*, London: Macmillan,
1890. PAGE 1 (border): Charles Folkard, *Songs from Alice*, London: A.&C. Black, 1929. PAGE 2 (background):
Unknown illustrator, n.d. CORNER INSET (throughout) and PAGE 12 (inset): Mabel Lucie Atwell, *AIW*,
London: Raphael Tuck, 1910. PAGE 17 (inset): Maggie Hinders. PAGE 109 (inset): Randolph Caldecott,
The Queen of Hearts, London: Routledge, 1881. PAGE 135 (inset): Willy Pogany, *AIW*, New York: Dutton,
1929. PAGE 145 (inset): Milo Winter, *AIW*, Chicago: Rand McNally, 1916. PAGE 160: John R. Neill,
Children's Stories That Never Grow Old, Chicago: Reilly & Lee, 1908.

Based on the book *All Things Alice* by Linda Sunshine,
published by Clarkson Potter/Publishers, Random House, Inc.
www.clarksonpotter.com
Printed in China
ISBN 978-0-307-35261-3